CHANGE THE GAME

*One Athlete's Thoughts on
Sports, Dreams, and Growing Up*

GRANT HILL

WARNER BOOKS

A Time Warner Company

Warner Books, Inc., 1271 Avenue of the Americas, New York, NY 10020
Visit our Web site at
http://pathfinder.com/twep

 A Time Warner Company

Printed in the United States of America
First Trade Printing: February 1997
10 9 8 7 6 5 4 3 2 1

Library of Congress Cataloging-in-Publication Data

Hill, Grant.
    Change the game : one athlete's thoughts on sports, dreams, and growing up / Grant Hill.
        p. cm.
    ISBN 0-446-67262-9
    1. Hill, Grant. 2. Basketball players—United States—Biography.
I. Title
GV884.H45A3 1996
796.323'092—dc20
[B]   95-49277
                                                                  CIP

Book design and composition by Giorgetta Bell McRee

*To my grandmothers, Vivian McDonald and
Elizabeth Hill*

ACKNOWLEDGMENTS

Several people's help was instrumental in completing this book. I'd like to thank them all: my parents, Janet and Calvin Hill; Tom George; Derrick Heggans; Sam Donnellon; Peter Sawyer; Rick Wolff; Lon Babby; and Bob Barnett.

CHANGE
THE GAME

THE GENERAL

Any book about me should start with my mother. I've often said that the woman I marry will be a lot like her. That tells you how much I admire my mom. It also tells you that I am a glutton for punishment.

My mom's name is Janet, but early on, one of my friends dubbed her "The General." Everyone liked my mother because she was very nice. But everyone feared her too. She could be tough, and she didn't care who you were. That continued all through high school and college and continues even today. Some of my friends who

Me (age 2) and my mother, Janet.

graduated last year even called my mother for job-hunting advice.

I am an only child. One of the reasons my parents give me for that is that I was a painful birth. I weighed over ten pounds and was twenty-two inches long. My body grew so quickly that I had to wear leg braces to bed when I was two to keep from becoming bowlegged. The doctor actually wanted to break both of my legs to straighten them out.

My mom said, "You're not breaking my baby's legs," and that was that.

Even doctors feared my mother.

I remember one time a friend of mine, Bobby Metz, came over to my house. My mom got mad at him for something. So she punished him by sending him to *my room*. She told him, "Go to Grant's room."

He cried and said, "I'm going to tell my mother."

My mom said, "Yeah, well I'm going to tell your mother too."

As I said, she could be tough.

My mom is very self-assured, very confident, very smart. I call her the Michael Jordan of mothers. Michael Jordan can do everything and is the best at everything he does. That's the way I look at my mother.

My mother expects the best too. Always. Growing up, it seemed I was always getting in trouble for something—little things that I thought were unfair.

My mother worked as a consultant at the

Pentagon when I was growing up in Reston, Virginia. Now she is a partner at Alexander and Associates, a Washington, D.C., consulting firm. Our neighborhood was upper-middle-class, and most of the mothers on the street stayed at home. I came home to a baby-sitter after school each day, and immediately made two calls.

The second was to my mother. The first was to the local pizza parlor.

The call to my mother was not voluntary. She asked direct questions about how my day went, and always told me what was going on in hers. I didn't always tell her everything about my life, but it didn't seem to matter. My mother knew everybody in town, she was the PTA president, and was very resourceful. You couldn't hide much from her.

If I came home from school and didn't call my mother a half-hour after school was out, I would be in trouble. If I didn't clean my room, I'd be in trouble. If I didn't get good grades, I'd be in trouble.

Looking back, it seems that I was always in trouble.

I was the type to want to do just enough to get by. If I got a B, to me that was okay. Not to my mom though. She taught me to give it my

Age 3 on vacation in Honolulu.

Age 9.

best effort, and not be satisfied unless it was my best.

She often did that through punishment. She would take away something I loved. I loved to eat. I remember once I called my grandmother—her mom—down in New Orleans when I was sent to my room without dinner. My grandmother loved to cook, and she loved me. She got on the phone and chewed my mother out. It was great. But when she hung up, I got punished some more.

When I got older, I got punished a lot for missing curfew. One time I came home late and my mom threw my new watch against a wall and it broke.

"You don't use it anyway," she said.

I felt bad about the watch, but worse because my mom was upset with me.

I sometimes used to get in trouble for lying. I'd get in trouble for doing something, and then in more trouble for lying about it. But then I got to the point where I realized if I didn't lie, I'd get punished. So why not try?

I could be bad at times. I never wanted to be on my mom's bad side though. That's not just because I feared her either. I loved her, and I didn't want to hurt her feelings.

In those days, I thought my mom was so unfair. By the time I went to college though, I realized that she had given me a great tool. All those years of getting into trouble and avoiding punishment taught me self-discipline. People talk about how hard it is to adjust to college. But for me, living at home with my mother was more difficult than college.

I don't know if I would be the same as a parent. I want to get my message across like my mother did, but I don't want to go to the extremes she did. It seems I was always being punished growing up. You hear a lot about kids who rebel against too much discipline, and turn out crazy. That didn't happen with me probably because there was a nice balance between my mom and dad.

My dad was a pushover compared to my mom. If he had a problem with something I did, he'd tell my mom, and she'd tell me. He would rarely confront me about something. I'm like my father that way.

It's funny, because a lot of my friends were afraid of my father growing up. His face can look mean even if he's just thinking. And he could go

*Me (age 2) and Mom. Look at my football jersey
with number 35—just like Dad.*

Age 2.

days without talking to you. But my dad never scared me. That was Mom's job.

My mother could be really nice too. She took me and three friends to Disney World once. That was great. I felt so cool, king of all kids. I did a lot of traveling when I was younger too. Egypt, England, Holland, France: I went all over the world. I loved it. I think I would have continued traveling all over the world while in high school and college had I not become serious about sports.

I was so involved in sports that I didn't really have the time to go on trips like that anymore. But in elementary school I went to a lot of different places and saw a lot of different things. At the time, I didn't always understand what I saw, which I regret. I wish there were some way I could have gone when I was in high school, but by then all my spare time was taken up with playing sports.

What I remember most about the trips was how much fun and how warm my mother was.

My mother was an only child too. So was my dad. Mom grew up in New Orleans in an upper-middle-class family. She was very prissy, very spoiled. Compared to my dad, she lived a very sheltered life. My dad grew up in Baltimore. He doesn't talk much about it, but I know he was working-class. Because of hard work and football, my dad went to a private school in New York for four years and then on to Yale.

My mom went to Wellesley College in Massachusetts, where she was a classmate of Hillary Rodham Clinton, who of course went on to become the nation's First Lady. My mom met my dad, I've been told a hundred times, at the Harvard-Yale game in 1968. Yale was undefeated in the Ivy League that year, and so was Harvard. The game ended in a 29–29 tie. But Yale was supposed to win. My dad, who did most of the scoring, considered it a loss.

It was at a party afterward that he met my mother. This seems almost miraculous to me. My dad played professional football for years, and he wasn't the easiest guy to talk to before games or after them. I can relate. Knowing how I feel following a loss, I can't imagine him being very glib following the game. I can't imagine my dad meeting the woman he would marry after a loss.

That's how it happened though. They were both seniors, and they married two years later. I came along two years after that, while my dad was playing for the Dallas Cowboys.

My name for the first few days of my life was "Baby Boy Hill." My parents had a few names they liked, but they went back and forth about each one. Finally Roger Staubach, the Cowboys quarterback, was so exhausted by their indecision that he said, "That's it. His name is Grant."

Typical quarterback—calling the play. I guess I owe him a big thank-you.

Grant Hill sounds much better than Baby Boy Hill.

THE DIPLOMAT

Losing all those games in my first season with the Detroit Pistons was tough. Until last season, I was always on winning teams. We lost more games last season than I had lost in all my years of playing basketball.

It was frustrating. But it was worse on my dad. I told you that he is easygoing, and he is—about everything except sports.

My dad was very sick over the winter. His blood pressure went down so much it scared my mom. My mom thinks he became so drained from watching eighty-two Pistons games on the satellite dish.

My dad, Calvin Hill, displaying his signature running style while playing for the Dallas Cowboys.

When my father watches sports, he mentally inserts himself into the game. That's with any sport. It is magnified, though, when his son is participating. My mom says he never learned how to be a fan, and I think she's right. I mean, he actually prepares himself before every one of my games. He even eats a pregame meal!

That comes from his years in pro football. Preparation was so important to him. He was so intense when he was on the football field that during the season you stayed away from him. For much of my childhood, my mother had to be both parents. Dad was there, but his mind was often somewhere else.

People think it must be so great to be the son of a professional athlete. In some ways it is. I was never bullied in school. I got invited to a lot of parties too. Compared to a lot of my friends, I had a very secure childhood and adolescence. But in some ways being the son of a professional athlete isn't so great.

There's a downside to it too. Due to the demands of his career, my dad missed out on certain aspects of my childhood. That was hard for me to understand as a kid. Now, as a professional athlete, I understand it completely. Athletes have egos and athletes have pride, but also, athletes who are good put a lot of hard work into what they do. And in doing that, you have to make sacrifices.

For fathers who are professional athletes, that sacrifice is usually giving up some time with their wives and children. Don't get me wrong. My dad still found time to spend with me. We often wrestled, threw the football in the backyard, and we must have gone to almost every major zoo in the country. He took me for rides on his bike, and we attended numerous Final Fours together. But when you're young, those moments seem few and far between. I think my mom was so tough on me because she was smart enough to realize she had to be. All of my dad's energy went toward being the best player he could be.

I experience it now. So much of your time and energy goes into your sport. That's true whether you are playing or just preparing yourself to play. Away from the field, you come home and you want to refresh yourself. You want to make sure when you go back out there, you are performing at a high level.

Dealing with a little kid? I can't even imagine that.

I couldn't have a kid right now. Maybe because

My dad, the ever-present fan.

I am immature, slightly. But also because I realize how much time is needed to raise children. When I come home, I want to relax. I want to go to sleep. I want to just do nothing, or do something that's relaxing and takes my mind off basketball.

Dealing with me as a child could not have been relaxing.

Especially when I was younger, having a professional athlete as a father was disconcerting. I wanted to fit in. I wanted the kids to know that I didn't think I was better than they were because my father was famous—that I was just like anyone else.

Sometimes, I was even embarrassed by my dad's success. In eighth grade, he came and spoke at my school. I didn't want him to come, and when he did, I faked like I was sick and went to the infirmary. I was not there for his entire speech. I was so uncomfortable he was even there. Most kids, if their parents were doing something very positive or unique, would feel kind of special. But I didn't want the success of my parents, what they had done, to shadow me. I didn't want people to judge me because of that.

I remember making my dad take me to my

basketball practices in a **VW** Bug instead of his Porsche. Funny thing is that he liked driving the Bug. I guess there were times he didn't like the attention either.

Dad started coming into the picture when I got into high school. By then his playing career was over, and he started attending all of my games. You hardly knew he was there. He's not a yeller or a screamer. But afterward, when I came back, there was always *the PGA*.

> I couldn't have a kid right now. Maybe because I am immature, slightly. But also because I realize how much time is needed to raise children.

That's "post-game analysis" for the uninitiated.

I would sit there in our home and he would go over the whole game: *I should have done this. I needed to work on that.*

Me (age 13) and my dad.

My mom thought it was so funny. She'd say, "Calvin, the boy had twenty-five points. Leave him alone."

But my dad was so intense. To him, my approach was too easygoing. Plus, I would purposefully act more uncaring than I really was in front of him.

I was rebelling. I didn't have a pregame routine because he did. Before a game in high school, I might be juggling a soccer ball, or playing out in the streets, or just running around the house. He would ask, "Aren't you going to lie down, put your feet up?"

If the game was at 7:30, I might not leave the house until 6:00. That drove him crazy. I would come into the house after playing outside, take a shower, and leave for the game. My father would say, "Where's the preparation? You've got to get mentally focused."

Later, at Duke, I understood how important that was. But in high school, there was none of that. We'd go to the game, and I'd be eating a sandwich on the ride there, or even in the locker room. Because he prepared so hard, I wanted him to think that it came easy for me. We won almost every game we played. We lost the state championship in the tournament every year, but we'd go through a season and maybe lose four games and win twenty-five. I was All-Met three years.

I worked at it of course. But I had to separate myself from him. That's also why I played basketball and soccer. My dad wouldn't let me play football when I was real young, but he fully expected me to get into the game when I got to junior high. Instead, I stuck with soccer. That was really my first love.

Only when it became apparent that basketball was my future—I was six feet when I was twelve—did I concentrate more on hoops. I never played football though. Still, I couldn't avoid being compared to or associated with my dad. I have a great relationship with the press now, but it didn't start out that way. No matter what I accomplished playing basketball in high school, my title was "Son of Ex-NFL Star Calvin Hill." I used to say, "Why do you guys always have to say something about my dad? When he was playing, you never mentioned *my* name."

I was really upset about that. It wasn't that I didn't appreciate my dad's accomplishments. I just wanted my accomplishments to be my own.

I probably owe my father a big thank-you though. As I got older, I became obsessed with trying to differentiate myself from him and what he had done. That's what drove me. Maybe I would have reached this point as an athlete anyway. I don't know. But he definitely was a factor.

When I got to college, one of my big goals was to do things that he hadn't. He was an All-American, but he didn't win a national championship. So I wanted to win a national championship. He won the NFL Rookie of the Year. Last year I said all year that Rookie of the Year didn't mean much to me, but that was a big fat lie. I couldn't go home and see his Rookie of the Year trophy and not see mine. If I hadn't won it, or shared it with Jason Kidd as I did, I probably wouldn't have gone home last summer. Now that we have both won Rookie of the Year awards my trading card sponsor, Skybox, is planning a joint Rookie of the Year card featuring both of us. That should be a first!

Once I beat my father in basketball, he wouldn't play me again. When I beat him in Ping-Pong, he wouldn't play me in that again either. Bowling? Same thing.

Some people get their competitive fire through brothers, or friends. I got it from my dad.

Just don't tell him that, okay? He'd never let me forget it.

HEALTHY, WEALTHY, AND WISE

loved being an only child.

I hated being an only child.

If you haven't already noticed, I sometimes contradict myself. As Walt Whitman said, "I am large, I contain multitudes." I think it goes back to wanting to be everyone's friend. I may have an opinion, but I usually understand both sides of an issue.

As an only child, I received all the attention and resources of both parents. In that way, I was spoiled. I traveled the world, went to Disney World, and received tons of love.

But I never had a brother, or a sister. There were no conversations as we lay in our beds at night, no teaming or scheming. Because my parents were both only children, I don't have any cousins, or aunts and uncles. I have a lot of friends who have big families, and sometimes we'd go to their family cookouts or gatherings. You see that, and it kind of makes you want to be there with a family the same size.

Would I be Grant Hill, NBA player, if I had been one of three, four, or five? Who knows? I do know that I've been blessed with the two parents I have. They were very strict on me growing up, but I also was given opportunities that other parents couldn't afford for their kids.

I think they presented a nice balance. Some kids of strict parents go a little haywire when they grow older. They have no rapport with their mom and dad, and that's real sad.

My parents presented choices. There were always two sides. I could be on their good side, or their bad side. I wanted to be on that good side, and I learned to sacrifice some of the things I wanted to do to stay on that good side. The good side allowed me to talk to them like a sibling, or a friend. I wanted to stay their friend. I've noticed

Basketball wasn't the only sport I played growing up.

At age 13 hamming it up for the camera with my friend
Michael Ellison.

as I've grown older and more responsible that Mom and Dad have kind of transformed into my best friends. I'm still their son, but when we get together now it's more like a meeting of old friends.

I'm lucky to have that. I thank God every day. But I also know there are people out there who are not as fortunate. I know there are kids and parents who will read this and say, "Yeah, well I don't have all that." The one thing they do have, though, is freedom of choice.

I have a lot of close friends who haven't had the same blessings, but still turned out to be good people. If guidance wasn't available at home, they found it somewhere. Or it found them. It wasn't easy. But there are always people—teachers, guidance counselors, coaches, social workers—who want to help you get through the tough times.

You've got to seek it though. I'll give you some examples.

Rob Robinson is one of my closest friends. He did not come from a wealthy family. I always knew of Rob, but we didn't know each other until we got to junior high. Even then, we were into different things. I wasn't really in with the cool crowd. Rob was, and he was very popular with the students. While Rob occasionally got into trouble, he was well received by everyone and people recognized his potential to excel.

> I know there are kids and parents who will read this and say, "Yeah, well I don't have all that." The one thing they do have, though, is freedom of choice.

Our paths never crossed until I was in eighth grade and he was in ninth. Because he was tall, six-three, the school guidance counselor pushed him toward the basketball team. Rob took to it pretty quickly, and he became the star pretty quickly too. It gave him confidence.

Everyone thought he was going to be the next great ballplayer at South Lakes High School. Jerome Scott, who went on to play at the

University of Miami, was a year older and he started on varsity. Everyone thought Rob would play varsity right away too.

The next year I was a freshman. I took Rob's spot on varsity. Rob would have made varsity if I hadn't come along. Rob could have been jealous but instead he supported me throughout the season.

He worked even harder in practice. The next year, and the year after that, with Rob now on the varsity team, we went on to the semifinals of the state tournament. Rob became a better student, and played well enough to earn a full scholarship to Niagara University. He graduated from college, and now he's playing professionally in Greece. When he finishes his career in basketball, he'll have a second career to look forward to.

Rob never did drugs, but some of those guys he hung with in his junior high days went on to do drugs in high school. A lot of them dropped out of high school.

Today Rob is someone just full of personality. He was at two games at the Palace this past season, and already he knows everyone there. He's got tickets for you, or courtside passes, or even press passes. I don't know how he gets them. He's very much the extrovert. You go out with him, he's going to talk to every girl he sees. He's got a lot of confidence, and he's great to be around.

He didn't have rich, doting parents. He wasn't an only child. He chose to surround himself with positive people. It doesn't have to be sports. But getting involved in something—yearbook, acting, social work—is a great way to build confidence and character.

The bottom line—no matter where you come from or your economic background—is to associate yourself with people interested in making your life better.

A LITTLE ABOUT LITTLE LEAGUE

Your parents, or guidance counselor, or coach, or teacher can only point the way. You've got to want to do it, and at least in sports, loving it is a pretty good idea too.

No kid is going to love a sport if a parent is hanging over them all the time. My dad lived his sports dream. Maybe because of that he stayed clear of offering advice until we began those PGAs in high school (remember? post-game analysis). By then I had developed a love for basketball that even he could not have rocked. But I developed it naturally, by playing and watching, and by listening to voices other than my father's.

By now we all know about the fathers who never fulfilled their sports dreams, and then try to live it through their sons. What happens almost always? Somewhere along the line, the kid drops the sport. I've even seen friends who were good, with real potential to play at a higher level, drop the sport.

Why? Because they never loved it. Their father loved it, coached them in it, and often drilled them about it. When you're ten, eleven, and twelve, the most important lesson you can learn in sports is to have fun. The rest comes later. If you love the sport you're playing, the fundamentals also come without a struggle. You don't *have* to get better. You *want* to get better.

When I was younger, I'd bounce the ball around the house, or I would go up the street to the neighbor's hoop and shoot all day and even at night until my mom would call me to come in. We had a sloped driveway so we never had a court. I had to rely on the generosity—and patience—of my neighbors to hone my skills.

As I mentioned, my dad showed no interest in soccer. And until high school, his interest in basketball consisted of sitting quietly in the stands. He wasn't there saying, "Okay, Grant, do this." I didn't have a parent hanging over me. I taught myself a lot of things. I would sit down and watch Georgetown games and see what they were doing and then go outside and try to do it myself.

> When you're ten, eleven, and twelve, the most important lesson you can learn in sports is to have fun.

I was nine or ten, just starting to play organized basketball. Because I was tall, the coach had me stand near the basket while someone else brought the ball up. Usually that was the coach's son, and he would take it up and shoot. I could dribble as well as anyone on the team, and I could shoot, but I wasn't getting the ball much. So one time, my dad said, "Grant, you go down and get the in-bounds and take it up the court." I started doing that, and then I started scoring. Pretty soon my job was to take the ball up the court.

My dad and I had a good laugh about it. They say all sons play for their fathers, and maybe that's true. But I played because it was fun. I never felt pressure from Dad. I loved the game and still love it. Even if I wasn't playing in the NBA, I'd be playing somewhere. I might have another job, but I would be playing basketball and enjoying it.

Look at Magic Johnson. As focused and as competitive as he is, he always seemed to have a big smile on his face. He had fun. Even now, in the NBA, the one thing I have to keep telling myself is that it's a game. It's a job, but it's also a game.

That's one thing Magic told me when I met him last January. He said, "Just go out and have fun and don't treat it as a job."

GROWING UP

Like any kid, I had problems with my father. They were problems neither of us could control.

In some ways I was uneasy with my dad's success. As a kid, I was real uncomfortable being the son of a professional athlete. I just wanted to fit in and be everyone's friend. I didn't want to think that I was better than anyone else, and I didn't want anyone else acting that way either.

Growing up in our little cul-de-sac, that wasn't a big problem. I was just one of the neighborhood kids. My grammar school, Terraset Elementary School, was through the woods behind my house.

My world was literally that school and that dead
end. There were twelve houses and kids in every
house. Kids of all ages too. We all seemed to play
with each other.

We were one of two Black families in our
upper-middle-class neighborhood. Because the
Washington Redskins practiced near there, a lot
of football players lived nearby. Among my dad's
close friends were Art Monk, Brig Owens, Ken
Houston, John Riggins, and Charley Taylor, and
they stopped by or we went to their homes from
time to time.

People in the neighborhood certainly knew
who my dad was. He was big stuff in those days.
But to the neighborhood kids, I was just someone
to play with, to add to a team or to tag if they
were "it." We played soccer in the dead end,
using driveways as goals. Or we played tag across
the entire neighborhood.

I moved there when I was three. Until the age
of ten, there didn't seem to be life outside that
cul-de-sac. The lone exception was soccer. I
would leave the neighborhood for practice, or for
camp in the summer. But that was it—school and
soccer and back home. Everyone was close, and
everyone looked out for each other. We'd get

together for barbecues in the summer. The kids would sleep over at each other's houses.

At the time I thought it was the best place in the whole world. I went back there recently, and it seemed so different to me. It was a nice sunny day on the weekend, and there were no kids. The school seemed run-down. Nothing stays the same I guess. Only your memories do.

TALL, DARK, AND INVISIBLE

Junior high was a shock for me. I went from outgoing to shy in the snap of a finger. When I got to seventh grade, I just totally changed. All the elementary schools in Reston were poured into this one school. I had lived this sheltered life up to this point, and all of a sudden, there was a little of everything.

Cliques sprang up overnight.

You had the cool people. You had the people who weren't cool. People who lived in the same neighborhood would run together. Or they would get into fights with kids from another neighborhood.

Me? I went into a shell. I just observed everything.

I blended in with the lockers. On purpose. I didn't want a group, a girlfriend, an identity. I was lucky too, because I never felt pressured that way. My dad was a pro football player. If I wanted to, I could hang with anybody. Or nobody.

A lot of the football players sent their kids off to private schools, and that was a big debate between my parents. My father had gone to that private school in New York for four years where he was one of a few Black kids, and it was a positive experience for him. It opened his eyes to all of the opportunities available if he worked hard.

As I said earlier, my mom was brought up in an upper-middle-class family. The Fairfax County school system was a good one, and it contained Black kids, White kids, Arab kids, Jewish kids, all types. Some were rich, some poor, some middle-class. Mom thought that diversity would not be available in private schools. She wanted me to have the opportunity to interact with all types of people.

Guess who won?

At first I didn't interact though. I enjoyed observing. That's how I rebelled. Here was this famous kid, who could have as many friends as he wanted, and he chose to have none. I came home every day and played soccer on the street with the fifth-graders. I was over six feet by then, and here I was playing with fifth graders. I could trust the old neighborhood.

Junior high? I was concerned that people liked me only because of whose son I was. I had a real problem with that, and I made it more difficult than it should have been. Also, I was afraid to smile when I was younger. My teeth were crooked—at least some people made me feel that way. My grandmother, who made false teeth, would always tell me, "You're going to need braces someday."

So I developed a complex about having crooked teeth and never smiled. I'm sure some kids thought I was stuck-up because of that, when it was actually the opposite.

Because they were working, my parents didn't know that I played with the little kids in the street. They were aware, though, that I wasn't bringing any friends home from school, or going to anyone's house. No one called. No one stayed overnight. I never went to the mall like the other kids. My mother became concerned that I was not a normal thirteen-year-old.

Dad and Mom began grilling me with questions. I remember one time we went to a Georgetown game and afterward my mother said, "You don't have any friends. How come no one is calling up here? Do you not have any friends in school?"

I wasn't unfriendly. I even had "school friends," kids I'd talk to while in school. But that was it. I remember there was this girl named Adrienne I had a big crush on. She was in a few of my classes, and she signed my eighth-grade yearbook. We sat next to each other in class, and for the most part we were cool. I'm not going to say we were friends, because we didn't socialize outside of class, but when we saw each other, we'd say hi.

She went to Mexico and came back, seven, eight years later. Now I'm nineteen, twenty years old and big stuff. I'm Grant Hill, the basketball player. And she didn't even remember who I was. I had to get the yearbook out and show her the picture. I showed her what she wrote, and she still didn't remember.

That shows you how I blended in with the lockers and everything else. I really enjoyed it too. There's a part of me even now that wishes I

Practicing with my high school team at age 14.

could still be back there, blending in. There was so much attention in high school, and then even more in college, that I became recognized no matter where I went in town. Last summer I came home to visit my parents, it's late at night and I'm waiting at the baggage claim, and a girl recognizes me and starts screaming, "Oh my God, it's you! It's you!"

It was embarrassing. I enjoy my fame mostly, but life was so much easier back in eighth grade. There was my schoolwork, soccer, and playing basketball. I didn't have to worry about all those other things that I have to worry about now.

When President Clinton was elected, he named my dad to the President's Council on Physical Fitness and Sports and we went to his swearing in at the Rose Garden. Later I took my parents to see Aretha Franklin perform there and we sat at the same table as Chelsea Clinton, the President's daughter. I thought about how easy I had it compared to her. She was only in junior high then, but she was already in the public eye as much as I was at Duke, if not more.

I remember what I was like at fourteen. She has it really rough.

THE EMERGENCE

My shy period signaled a growing interest in basketball—and girls. Actually, the two interests seemed to intertwine like, well, a net.

I'll explain.

As you know, because our driveway had a slope, I had to find other driveways with baskets to practice at. Through the woods, on the next block, was a girl I had a big crush on, and her neighbors had a hoop with lights and a Plexiglas backboard. There were few things cooler to a kid in those days than a Plexiglas backboard, but for me, Ellen Butler might have been one.

*With my dad and former Georgetown University star
Michael Jackson, who played with Sacramento and is now
with Turner Sports in Atlanta.*

So when the weather was warm and I had done my homework, or school was out, you would find me out there shooting, shooting, shooting—and hoping she would come out of her house for a glimpse. Sometimes she would even say hi and I would say hi back.

For me in those days, that was pretty intense.

Basketball had become intense too. When I had a chance to make a traveling AAU (Amateur Athletic Union) team in seventh grade, I abandoned my first love, soccer, to concentrate on hoops. My coach was a gentleman named Jim Warren, who had played with Jerry West at West Virginia many moons before.

Coach Warren had coached the Northern Virginia Hawks for two decades before I showed up. He coached guys who became great college players, and some pros too. He ran complicated offenses, college offenses, and really schooled you in how the game was meant to be played.

Coach Warren was a disciplinarian and he worked us hard. He would call me Moses, after Moses Malone, because I was the big man inside. He had this two-handed set shot right out of one of those old-time films, and he'd always beat me at H-O-R-S-E with it.

We were never the most talented AAU team when it got to the national tournament. We were always the best-coached. My mom dubbed us "The Surgeons" because of the way we could pick teams apart. I played with Randolph Childress, who went on to star with Wake Forest and is now with the Portland Trail Blazers. We won the tournament when I was in the eighth grade, and we beat teams that included such future stars as Chris Webber, Jamal Mashburn, and Glenn Robinson.

What a shot of confidence that was, especially entering high school! I tended to doubt myself a lot in those days, and I felt in awe of people easily. That's where my dad helped a lot. I would come home and talk about how good one player was, and he'd say, "Grant, you're better than him." Deep down I knew that, but when my father said it, all doubt was erased.

Every father should do that. It should be put in a job description somewhere. I'm always amazed when a father downgrades his own kid, or calls him names in front of people. Whose side is he on?

Anyway, buoyed by that AAU championship, I won a spot on the varsity squad in my freshman

Playing one-on-one with my dad at age 15.

year of high school. I averaged fourteen points
that year and received my first letter from a college. Denny Crum, coach of Louisville, sent it.

> I'm always amazed when a
> father downgrades his own kid,
> or calls him names in front of
> people. Whose side is he on?

I exploded my sophomore year. By then I was
six-six, and I could dunk. There was this playground in Reston called Twin Branches and all
the good players from the area assembled there
during the summer for memorable days of pickup
games. It produced players like Michael Jackson,
who went on to Georgetown and the NBA, and
Dennis Scott, who's now with Orlando. And it
produced me.

Probably the first big name to come from
that playground was Carlos Yates. When I was
five or six, I remember watching my dad play

with Carlos. A little later, Michael Jackson came along. He was The Man for a long time, a real teen idol, and I knew everything about him. I knew his favorite song. He used to drive this tan Z28. He used to have the prettiest girlfriend. He went to Georgetown, my favorite team growing up.

When he came back home it was a real event.

Carlos Yates never made it past college, and he didn't have much to fall back on. A few years after college he was shot and killed in D.C. Michael, however, is a business success because he did more than just play basketball in college. No matter how good you are—or think you are—you should always hit the books. There are many more lawyers, doctors, and consultants out there than professional athletes. And most are doing quite well.

After Michael Jackson, Dennis Scott came along and went to the next level. He could dunk and shoot from the outside as well as handle the ball. He went to Flint Hill Academy, which was ranked as the best high school basketball team in the country by *USA Today*. By the time he was a senior, he was the best player that playground had ever seen.

Dennis left for college after my freshman year, and I became The Man at Twin Branches. Meanwhile, our high school team never lost more than four games in a season and while we never won a state championship, we made it within a game or two each year.

The team revolved around me. My high school coach, Wendell Byrd, didn't limit me either. Because I was the tallest, my role was often to play with my back to the basket. But Coach Byrd also let me bring the ball up and shoot from the perimeter. Until then, I would do those things only on the playground.

Coach Byrd gave me the opportunity and confidence to try them for real, and I improved every game because of that. I will be forever grateful.

THE PROCESS

I never thought much about the pros in those days. For me, making it was playing for a major college. The Washington Bullets were the NBA and they were bad. Georgetown was a major college, which at the time featured my idol, star player Michael Jackson. They were, and still are, one of the best programs in college basketball.

My mom was a big fan of Georgetown coach John Thompson. My dad loved North Carolina. At different times during high school, I was absolutely sure that I was headed to each.

Georgetown was the first. A lot has been made

As a member of the McDonald's High School All-American team. In uniform: (standing left to right) Melvin Simon, Ed O'Bannon, Shawn Bradley, Eric Montross, Anthony Cade, Kendrick Warren, (kneeling left to right) Darrin Hancock, Jamie Brandon, Damon Bailey, and Grant Hill.

already of my disastrous interview there, when I was told to read from a book to Coach Thompson's academic advisor, Mary Fenlon. Apparently all student athletes who visit Georgetown, no matter who they are, are asked to participate in this reading exercise. And while, at the time, I was offended, I now understand and appreciate the purpose for such an exercise. Coach Thompson cares about developing the minds of those who play for him. This is evident in the graduation rate of Georgetown basketball players. The truth is that Georgetown was too close to my home for me to go there anyway. My parents would have been there every game and every weekend. I'd get a PGA every game. The way my mother is, I'd probably still get punished too!

I was pretty sure, though, that I wanted to go to Carolina. I loved everything I heard and saw about the school. It was far enough away, but not too far.

Duke? I hated Duke.

I can't even tell you why I decided to visit there. Even when I was down there, I remember calling the sister of one of my friends at Carolina. She asked, "Are you thinking about going there?" And I said, "No way."

Age 17 at my high school graduation with my parents and grandmothers.

That was before I met and spoke with Mike Krzyzewski, the Duke coach. I was recruited heavily, and up to that point virtually every coach assured me of a starting job as a freshman. Coach K went the other way. He told me there was a lot of talent on the team, and that he hoped to add as much talent while I was there as he could. I would earn my minutes, he said, and I would earn starting status.

Or I would not. It was all up to me.

I was hooked. I didn't make another visit after that. I was a Blue Devil.

THE HUXTABLES

Bigotry can be blatant and it can be subtle. Last year, for example, a magazine article appeared that asked, "Can Grant Hill Save Sports?" Most people, even my mother, saw it as a positive article. It complimented me for being smart, unassuming, and modest. Along with such praise, though, were some troubling characterizations.

The writer of the article described a party I went to. There were some guys wearing fur coats who made a big deal over me, and the writer described me at one point as "the king of the hoodlums." The implication to me and most of my friends was that "hoodlum" equaled "Black." Take me out of that scene, a friend pointed out, and it paints an unfair and unflattering picture of African-American men.

Too sensitive? I don't think so. Here's another example. Sometimes my family is described as the "Huxtables" after the Bill Cosby show of a few years ago. In the show both parents have good jobs. They have good children. I should take such a comparison as a compliment, right?

Hold on. When a big deal is made of my background, what is implied is that Black people can't have that. Or at least, that my family is not normal for Black people.

Maybe we aren't. Black, white, brown, or yellow, my parents are not normal. They are exceptional people who have worked hard for their success. I had tremendous advantages over most Black families growing up.

I had tremendous advantages over most White families too.

It works the other way too sometimes. When African-Americans become successful, to some Blacks they automatically become White. Everything they do, from the car they buy to the clothes they wear, is analyzed in that vein.

The first day of school my freshman year at Duke University. From left to right: Eurol Lang, me, Andre Lang, and Tony Lang, my roommate.

As a kid my mom drilled me on the correct use of English, and now I have a good command of the language. Because of that, I'm not Black enough for some members of my race. Well, I've been Black all my life. I speak the way I was taught to speak. But if you pronounce your words a certain way, or you dress a certain way, then to some you're not "down." You're not acting "Black."

> I had tremendous advantages over most Black families growing up.
> I had tremendous advantages over most White families too.

If I'm going to be a role model, I want to be an inspiration to all children. Maybe I provide more inspiration to Black children than others—I don't know. But that doesn't mean I don't try to have a positive effect on all.

My parents.

Maybe I can even help wash out some of those hard lines that have been drawn between the races. It sure would solve a lot of problems.

Once I was asked in an interview about the woman of my dreams, my ideal. I made a lot of comparisons to my mother. The interviewer, who was White, said, "This lady would be African-American, right?" I found this question to be inappropriate. No matter what I said, someone was bound to be offended. Thinking real fast, I said, "Marriage? I can't even imagine being married." I made light of it. Had I said "yes," I would have been considered biased against those who are not African-American. If I had said "no," or "not necessarily," some Black people might have taken offense.

One thing I take pride in is that I've been able to blend. I can be in a White environment and get along fine, and I can be in an all-Black environment, in the middle of a city, and get along fine too. I'm the same person no matter where I am. I don't go "Yo, what's up?" in the city, because that's not me. And I don't speak any more refined in an upscale setting, because I'm not that way either.

Growing up where I did, I had a nice mix. Even the mix of friends I have now. Some are—or were—more well-off than I am and some are not. We all come from different backgrounds.

I just try to be myself wherever I am. Most people seem to respect that. And if they don't, it's their problem, not mine.

COACH K

For us to win in high school, I had to do everything. In my senior year I averaged thirty points, twelve rebounds, and eight assists, and it came easily.

College? A whole different story there.

I was called a reluctant star during my first two seasons at Duke. I had talent, but I only wanted to fit in. That was the knock.

I'd like to say it wasn't true, but it was. I was in awe when I got to Duke. All of a sudden these guys I'm watching on national television all the time—and Duke was on a lot—are playing with

*Hugging my mother during my jersey retirement ceremony at Duke's
Cameron Indoor Stadium. Coach K and my dad look on.*

me and against me. My very first day of pickup there, I got dunked on by Christian Laettner of all people. I went back to the dorm, called my dad and said, "I don't know if I'm good enough to be at this level."

He assured me that I was. Our relationship changed for the better when I was at Duke. Now, I wanted to listen to him! I wanted to hear his PGA, his reassuring voice, his philosophy. All my life, I have tended to doubt myself when facing a stiff challenge. All my life, my dad has been able to eliminate those doubts.

In Coach K, he had a lot of help. Coach taught me how to win. I always wanted to be a winner, but I didn't know exactly how to win. That's like saying you want to do well in school. Someone has to show you how many hours you have to put into studying, how to budget your time, how to get your rest, how to prepare for tests.

My dad always talked about preparation, but I was too young when he was a player to remember his example. Sometimes too, hearing it from someone else makes it all click.

Coach K was that click. Just by watching him, he taught me about focus and preparation and fortitude. In high school, I showed up and just tried to play my best. Practice wasn't that important. To Coach K, though, practice was paramount.

He taught me that it was okay to try and dominate a game as long as it was in the confines of team play. He liked to say, "Don't be afraid to be great." He told me that for four years, but I learned it as much from watching him as I did from listening to him.

No matter what situation we were in, he was confident. In my sophomore year, we were down to Kentucky by two with two seconds left in the regional final. We all came to the huddle still burned by the shot that put Kentucky up, and Coach K had a plan already mapped out on the board. He said, "Okay, here's how we win the game: Grant, you throw to Christian here and he'll take the shot to win." And that's exactly how it happened. We went on to win the NCAA title.

I really learned a lot about not quitting from that game, about how to carry yourself so your opponent doesn't see your emotions. They were things my father would always talk about when I was in high school. Maybe I was too young, too brash, too immature then. When I struggled in college, though, I called home for his advice often.

Surrounded by classmates at my college graduation.

In a lot of ways, my college success mirrored high school. I started freshman year—I guess I was good enough, huh?—and we won the National Championship. We won it again my sophomore year, and I had an even bigger role. That might have been my best year in college. I had a lot of spectacular plays. Christian was definitely The Man, and that freed me up quite a bit.

When the ball was in the half-court, the goal was to try and get it to Christian. The only way we could score was to play good transitional defense and score off turnovers and fast breaks. If we could get the defensive rebound and push it up the floor quickly, we didn't have to play the half-court offense.

That kept all the egos in check, and they were ample on that team. Defense became almost more important than offense—we used to actually get angry if a team scored on us. I remember one game against Boston University up there. We weren't that deep, and the second string went in and gave up a big lead. The next day Coach K read the bench players the riot act. He said, "You haven't earned your minutes, you're terrible, all the rewards you have are because of the starters. I'm not going to give you any more minutes until you prove yourself in practice. I'll play the starters forty minutes a game."

We heard that and we were like little kids who had been promised an unlimited supply of birthday cake.

Forty minutes? Our eyes popped open. In practice, the first string plays against the second string. The next day the starters—Thomas Hill, Brian Davis, Bobby Hurley, Christian, and me—are talking among ourselves and saying, "Let's kick their butts." We wanted to play forty minutes a game so badly that we went out there and beat up on them. Our teammates. Our friends. They couldn't score, dribble, or do much of anything.

That was the best year. No matter who we played against, when we stepped on the court we were so confident. We relied on each other so much, we trusted each other so much. That was the best feeling, knowing that we were going to win every time out.

ROCK STARS

I told you Duke was on television a lot when I was in high school. That didn't change once I got there either. We went to three Final Fours in my four years there, and we were on national television more than most NBA teams were.

We became famous because of it too. The Final Four is an unbelievable scene in terms of media coverage. Cameras follow you everywhere, and every practice is monitored by what seems to be a thousand reporters and a couple hundred cameras. To survive, you have to act comfortably in front of a camera. I wasn't very good at it when I got there. But I was an artist by the time I left.

For the first two seasons at Duke, it was easy. We had Christian and Bobby, and they became like rock stars. They were hounded by groupies in every town we visited. Christian had it worse. Teenage girls would come to the hotel and hang out, or try to call his room, or wait outside of practice. We'd go to an arena, and there would be girls screaming at Christian, crowding around him. It was like that for Bobby too, but he was like the drummer. Christian was lead vocalist.

Television made it that way, I'm convinced. Those two became more recognizable than most NBA stars, and they had to learn quickly how to present themselves on camera, and protect their time away from the game.

Christian could be a real artist that way. He was a great interview, really sold you on that choirboy, All-American image. Off camera though, he was a rascal, and he could really ride you when the mood struck him. He was undoubtedly our leader, though, and he handled the media heat well.

Coach K reminded us often that we represented Duke as much as ourselves when the cameras, pads, and pens came around, and to act accordingly. Problem was, the cameras, pads, and pens always seemed to be around.

I think we became even tighter because of that. Certainly it led to one of the more unusual time-killing games I've ever heard of for a team. A few guys, myself included, had been forced to learn piano when we were younger. We all had songs that we had mastered through the years, and when we hit the hotel and had time, we'd head for the lobby piano.

Quickly, we got sick of each other's songs. Now we were competing to see who could master new songs. The more challenging your song, the more impressive you were. Christian was the best—surprise—but I held my own. The best part was that I was playing piano again and enjoying it.

Last season I went on the David Letterman show and played with the band. My mom, who has played all her life, was so proud.

I guess I owe a debt of thanks to Christian.

The Rock Star.

THE MAN

Christian graduated after my sophomore year and went off to the NBA. Because of that, and because I was hurt for the first time in my career, junior year was a rough one.

It started off great. I was oozing confidence after playing well against the Dream Team the summer before, and played well in the early part of the schedule. I averaged twenty points and the team was also doing well. Christian had received a lot of the credit for our two championships. We were out to prove it wasn't just him.

Handling the ball my freshman year against Georgetown.

In late January I landed hard on the ball of my foot during practice, and the trouble began.

At first it didn't feel so bad. So I kept playing. But in February, while jumping for a ball, I landed on the ball of the foot and a couple of other feet landed on it as well, and I knew it was bad. I broke several bones between the ball of the foot and the toe, and also tore some ligaments. That's the clinical description. The basketball player description is this: I messed it up bad.

For the rest of the regular season, I sat. I came back for the postseason, but that didn't last too long. We lost the first game of the ACC (Atlantic Coast Conference) Tournament, and lost in the second round of the NCAA tournament to California, who had some guy named Jason Kidd.

Duke's string of NCAA titles had ended. I felt more than a little responsible.

The foot was operated on after exams that spring, and I spent June and July on crutches. My cast didn't come off until August. I didn't resume playing basketball again until September, a layoff of nearly six months.

I was twenty then. I had played basketball twelve months of the year for nearly a decade. I came back to school, met with reporters, and did what any athlete in my position would do.

I guaranteed a national championship.

Duke wasn't supposed to go anywhere that year. Bobby had graduated, Thomas Hill had graduated. Antonio Lang, like me, was coming off a disappointing year. Cherokee Parks had a difficult task of replacing Christian, and we had no proven guards. North Carolina, having just won the national title, had most of their guys back and had an excellent class of recruits.

I had a great time with the writers. I told them we would be "The Silent Assassins," sneaking up on everyone. Rather than rust me, the six months off had refreshed me. I had a lot of time to think, and I thought a lot about my shortcomings as a team leader. "Don't be afraid to be great," Coach said. Well, this year I was going to be great.

My attitude all senior year was the same attitude Coach K showed during that Kentucky game two years before. I was not going to let my team lose. And we didn't lose, at least not much. I led the team in points, assists, and steals, and we rolled all the way to the championship game against Arkansas, which had spent most of the season ranked number one.

Holding my newly retired jersey, which now hangs from the rafters at Duke's Cameron Indoor Stadium.

I had a blast with the media at the Final Four, especially the ones from North Carolina who were around for my big boast the summer before. It was not like me to do something like that, and when it happened, it became like an inside joke. Like *We're here. Can you believe it?*

I was convinced by then we were for real, though. I was crushed when Arkansas beat us in the final game to win the championship. I remember Coach K told us in the locker room afterward how great we played and that we had nothing to be ashamed of. And I was mad at him for that! He was my guru. *Don't be afraid to be great.*

Now, of course, I see that season as a great accomplishment. We weren't the most talented team by far, but we played with focus, toughness, and unbridled confidence.

We weren't afraid to be great, and so we were.

Well, almost.

FAME

I miss my sleep.

When I came home from college, I could go to sleep late and sleep until noon or 1:00. Many times, family legend has it, my father would go upstairs and put a mirror under my nose just to make sure I was breathing. I slept ten, twelve hours straight in those days.

I get tired just thinking about it.

Now, seven hours is about the most sleep I get in one night. Besides my job with the Pistons, I run a company called GranHco, which oversees my various commercial and endorsement deals.

*Posing with two participants in the North Carolina
Special Olympics.*

It's like having two jobs, but I'm not complaining. I'm young. I have the energy.

And I guess I don't *need* more than seven hours of sleep. The problem is, my body doesn't know when to sleep anymore. When we play night games, I'm so pumped with adrenaline afterward that it takes me hours before I get to sleep. The next morning there's usually practice, and your body's working again. Or worse, there's a shootaround, and another game that night.

That's the NBA in a nutshell. An eighty-two-game sprint toward total exhaustion. Get up early, stay up late, pack your bags, and jump in a plane every two days or so. Losing as many games as we did last season also takes it toll.

Even when you have a day off, your body is so messed up it can't adjust. I haven't had a great night's sleep in a long time.

I know, I know—Boo-hoo-hoo. Poor little millionaire. You're right. Who can complain about a job you love, that pays so well, and treats you like royalty everywhere you go?

Yet that's what's happening in professional sports—athletes are complaining. It's not just in the NBA, although we've received most of the publicity. We've got guys challenging their coaches in public, guys missing practice and games, guys pouting about their minutes or about their teammates—all in the newspaper and on TV.

I don't need to name names. You just had to pick up a newspaper during the last couple of NBA seasons.

Celebrity is a privilege. It is not a right. You earn it in some way. And with it comes a serious obligation to those who give you the celebrity. It's not just vested in you. It has to be because of talent, or because as a political leader you're going to bring something to us. Or as an entertainer, you're going to be on the TV screen. There's a giveback, and I understand that. I saw that in my dad, and in some of the politicians I've met through my mom's work, and through some friends.

People have bestowed a certain power on me through their admiration that the twenty-three-year-old next door doesn't have. And she or he might have tons to offer. But the public doesn't know of him or her like they know of me.

Is that fair? Is that right? I don't know, probably not. But if you don't abuse that power, or you use it to help, it doesn't have to be bad . . .

Let's face it. All athletes like attention. Glenn Robinson may say he doesn't, but he at least has an ego. And when he's done playing, I'll bet he'll miss seeing his name in print. I saw that happen to my dad, and his persona with the media was much like Glenn's. I think that's why I like Glenn so much. He reminds me of my dad.

It was tough on my dad when he retired. It took him something like three years to get over it and move on—to really just let go of it. He was moody. His head was ready to play, but his body wouldn't let him. And I know when that day comes for me it will be tough.

Celebrity is a privilege. It is not a right.

You see it in my dad through me. He's told me that my experience as a college and pro athlete has made him feel reincarnated as a celebrity. People call him for interviews again. He's asked his opinion at games. For the most part, he loves it.

For the most part, I love my celebrity too, but there's always a price. I'm trying to be more conscious or aware of how my people react to Black professional athletes. Or Black superstars. There's this perception that when someone Black makes it in the world of sports or entertainment, that they forget who they are. And in some cases that's correct, but in some cases it's unfair.

I could go and do all this charity work and give back to the community, and still you would find people out there who are not satisfied. They will say I am not doing enough for the Black community. But you can do only so much. You have to be part of the world, and the world is not all Black.

Look at Michael Jordan. People say he doesn't speak up or use his power to do what he wants. And Magic Johnson too. You hear it all the time: They could be doing so much more. Both do a lot, but to paraphrase former President Abraham Lincoln: "You can please some of the people all of the time. You can please all of the people some of the time. But you cannot please all of the people all of the time."

I'm not a confrontational person. Never have been, never will be. If I'm going to have a positive effect on the world, it won't be through controversial speeches or politicking. I'm more of an ambassador. I see myself visiting schools, financing education programs like the one we began in Detroit, trying to have a say in the lives of as many kids as I can. I'd like to be part of a rescue team for kids looking for a way out.

There will be times, I am sure, when there will be issues I get involved in, and when there will be controversy in my life. I even prepare for it like I do basketball: I imagine sticky situations all the time and ponder how I would solve them. I look at something that's happened to another player. How would I handle that if the same thing happened to me? I don't know if that's fear or just wanting to be prepared.

Probably a little bit of both . . .

There's going to be controversy. I know it. Everything this year has been good.

Maybe that's why I don't sleep as well. I'm a big boy now, with an active mind. My bedroom at my parents' house whistles when the wind blows. In all my years in high school and college, I never noticed that. I slept right through it.

Now it keeps me up all night.

FALSE PROMISE

Even when your heart is in the right place, celebrity can be prickly. Especially when it's new to you.

Amid all my Rookie of the Year exposure last season, I went to a school in Detroit to speak about education. I told the kids about how I had dreamed of being an NBA athlete, and I told them how hard I worked in school to get good grades in the likely case my dream did not work out. I used this analogy: When you jump out of an airplane, you jump out with two parachutes. If that first one doesn't work, you always have that second parachute that you can rely on.

For me, academics was that second parachute.

The next day my words were printed in the newspaper, and a critical editorial was written. I emphasized sports ahead of education, it said, and that's wrong. My point was to leave yourself a second option so that your dream, if broken, won't result in a crash down to earth. You have two parachutes. You're covered.

> When you jump out of an airplane, you jump out with two parachutes.

I learned something there. When you're in the public eye, people are going to scrutinize everything about you. Especially when you present yourself as a role model, which I do. Hey, I scrutinize celebrities myself.

But my point that day was valid. The older you get, the more your dream should be rooted in reality. It has to be attainable. There are a lot of players in the CBA (Continental Basketball

Association) who are not even stars or starters, just role players still chasing their NBA dreams. There comes a time when you have to jump out of yourself and look at it objectively: "Okay, is there even a chance of this happening?"

I said earlier in the book that I would play basketball even if I didn't make the NBA. And I would. But I'd have another job.

Everyone has a dream. Sometimes, though, people have to give up on that dream or their life goes nowhere. A dream should inspire you. When it becomes a crutch, an escape, it's time to leave it behind.

There are a lot of great basketball players out there. There are a lot of great basketball players just on the courts at Twin Branches. They probably look at me and think, "A couple of breaks, a little more work, and I could have been him."

Making it to professional basketball involves a lot of luck. Sure I put a lot of hard work into it, but there were friends of mine who put the same amount of work into it and never even played in college. You need work, and you need God-given talent, and then on top of that you need inspired guidance. I had an abundance of all three things and made it. But for every me, there are a hundred thousand guys whose dreams dissipate because they come up short in one or all of those categories.

I'll go to basketball camps now and I'll say, "How many of you guys want to play in the NBA?" Every single one of them will raise their hands. How many guys want to go play in college? How many guys want to start on your varsity team in high school? The hands stay up.

Then I'll say, "Ten of you guys, out of two hundred, will play varsity basketball in high school. If you're lucky, one of you guys might play Division I college basketball. Those are the odds—maybe even less than that. That one person may have a chance at one of the three hundred NBA jobs, although the odds again say probably not."

Every time I do this, kids stare at me dumbfounded. They don't realize that. I tell them, "The danger is not in wanting to be like your heroes. The danger is in forgetting everything else to chase that. A dream is just that: something to shoot for. Arms in the sky, feet planted in reality."

Have another parachute. Have as many parachutes as you can. Then chase your dream with all your heart.

CHANGE THE GAME

For the most part, I have a good rapport with people in my profession. I get along with teammates, most opponents, and fans.

The formula is simple. Treat others with the respect you would like for yourself. Reporters have a job to do, so I set aside time for them. A coach, like your boss, needs to be heard and heeded.

When I dunk, I don't point my finger, or get in someone's face. I guess this makes me different from a lot of guys in the NBA, but I've never derived pleasure from making someone else feel bad or angry. That probably goes back to wanting to be everyone's friend. When the game's over, I don't want guys on the other team to hate me.

That's why this whole comparison with Glenn Robinson hurts me. Apparently one of us has to be the bad guy. Because Glenn held out for a big contract with Milwaukee and I signed for less, he's perceived by some as greedy and I'm not.

We're both good basketball players. I don't know if the similarities end there, but so what if they do? I may be perceived as more outgoing than Glenn, but again, so what?

We're friends and we're rivals. Unfortunately the two of us have been pitted against each other through the media. I hope we can get over that. Glenn's a great guy and a great player.

Don't get me wrong. I enjoy beating a guy to the ball, or dunking on him. And I'm excited when I do. I may even pump my fist. That's a celebration of my success, and my team's success. This game is about competition, matchups, and winning all the little wars. When I step out there, I want badly to beat you. But I don't have to put you down to do it.

Right now, that may seem to be a minority opinion on some NBA teams, and for some com-

*With David Robinson before practicing against
Dream Team I.*

Father and son.

panies promoting those athletes. It's like, "Boorish is beautiful." I know people have been turned off by some bad behavior over the last couple years. To be honest, I have too.

Sorry, no names. Promoting myself at the expense of others is the same as pointing a finger after a dunk. That's not me, and it's not what this book is about. I'd like to see respect come back in vogue in the NBA, but the only way to do that is through example. Try to tell someone to do something, the knee-jerk reaction will likely be, "Who does he think he is?" Lead by example, and you've got a better chance.

I know I've been given the role of savior. After that magazine article, I may even apply for sainthood. The NBA too has bestowed its promotional blessings on me. There are some people out there who even believe that the Rookie of the Year honor I shared with Jason Kidd of Dallas was orchestrated by the league. I don't know how. It's based on a vote. But it shows you the kind of spotlight I'm under.

I think I'm just in the right place at the right time. A couple of years ago, you had the Dream Team. Magic Johnson was still playing. Larry Bird was still playing. I could have slipped into the NBA with much less fanfare.

But the league has taken a big hit in the last few years because of a few boorish stars. It has been criticized, and in some places it has lost some popularity. I think they see me as a chance to start over. It's a hot and uncomfortable spotlight sometimes, but the upside has been tremendous. In my eyes, I haven't done a thing yet in the NBA, yet I have the security of a nice contract, as many endorsements and appearances as time will allow, and even my own line of clothing with FILA.

The FILA people have been great. Howe Burch, a vice president at FILA, has made me its promotional star, and the commercials are honest and positive. That's what *Change the Game* is all about. You can be a competitor, a gamer, a winner, and you can show some respect too.

ROLE MODEL

I remember when Magic Johnson announced he was HIV positive in the autumn of 1991. I was a sophomore at Duke, and we had just finished a preseason practice. On my way to the training table, I saw a friend's dorm room packed with people, so I ducked inside.

There's Magic, on TV, announcing that he had the virus that causes AIDS. I'll never forget how quiet that room became, or the meal that followed. Most in that room and at the training table idolized Magic, and not just because he was a great basketball player. He had been its ambassador for more than a decade, pumping out positive messages to kids like me as I grew up. Now, it was almost as if he had died. Everyone was just so silent, like you are when in shock.

Like it or not—and it's a little of both for me—I hold that kind of power now. I show up at the baggage claim that night, and that woman starts screaming. I go to all these NBA cities, and because I'm in commercials, people cry out to me as if they know me. Part of you realizes that it's good to make someone feel that way, so excited. But you also want to shake that person and say, "Calm down, relax, it's just another person." I don't want to come down on those fans, but there's a right place. I want to be approachable, but I also want to eat my dinner in peace at a restaurant.

Still, I sign my autograph anytime someone comes over to my table. Instead of being unpleasant or aloof, I choose to be friendly. As professional athletes, we have two choices: We can resist or abuse such power, or we can use it to make positive change.

Parents are the best role models. For those without either or both parents, counselors, Big Brothers/Big Sisters, or anyone you respect and trust are the next best thing.

Having said that, I also realize that my words and actions, and the words and actions of other athletes, hold a lot of importance. Far too much importance. We're not poets, philosophers, or statesmen. I shoot a ball through a hoop for a living.

But a lot of people, and especially kids, will listen to someone like me before they will listen to their local congressman. That's the way society is. It's unbelievable power.

I'd like to make positive change. I'd like to be a role model. I'd like to inspire people like Arthur Ashe did, or Julius Erving did, or even Magic did.

> We're not poets, philosophers, or statesmen. I shoot a ball through a hoop for a living.

I wasn't a tennis buff, and Ashe played before my time. But after I read his book *Days of Grace* in college, I really respected the things he did, and what he stood for. I think he's still the last top ten American tennis player to graduate from college. It was important for him to get his degree from UCLA, just as it was for me to get mine from Duke.

I respect Dr. J so much for so many reasons too. He was a businessman from day one of his career. It's funny that as flashy a player as he was, he was very down-to-earth when it came to money. I like to think I'm that way too. I'm an extrovert and I've got my mom's gift for gab, but I'm as conservative with my money as my dad was. Well, maybe not as conservative. My dad has a fleet of cars in his driveway, and sometimes people will see this as flashing wealth. But take a better look. He's got every car he's ever owned in that driveway, from that VW Bug right on down. My dad doesn't throw anything away, not even his old cars.

Of course I've already made more than my father did in his entire career with the Cowboys, Redskins, and Browns. With ESPN and all the commercial opportunities out there, professional sports is different from when he played. Here I am, barely twenty-three, and I have a sneaker and line of clothing named after me, I am a spokesman for FILA, GMC Trucks, Kellogg's, and Sprite and I'm in demand for a lot of things. I've been on *20/20,* at least one magazine has anointed me the savior of all sports, and I really haven't done a thing!

It's just a little overwhelming.

Truth is, I'm just trying to help save the Pistons. Potentially I can be a leader, and I would like to be someone that kids can look to as a man of principle and example: a public figure.

I look at it like, "Who wouldn't want that?" Not everyone gets this opportunity. There is responsibility, and pressure, but there's also a power to change or improve people's lives. I want that burden.

That's something I had to say about a year ago when my parents, attorneys, and advisors met to discuss what direction we wanted to go with GranHco and my marketing strategy. The question came up, "Do I want the pressures that Michael Jordan has?" I'm not another Michael Jordan. But from a marketing standpoint, I am canvassing a lot of the same ground that he has. Endorsing products, making appearances, fulfilling obligations—some players don't want that. But I said then, and I still feel this way: "Hey, I want to have Michael Jordan's problems."

I have big plans. I want to do a lot. I want to be remembered. I want to be a great player, and I want to use that status to do a lot of positive things.

There's a price, of course. Just going out to the store for milk can turn into an autograph session. But it comes with the territory. I can't say I want to be all this, without the baggage that comes with it.

I just had this house built in Detroit. It's big—my mom calls it my starter home—but part of the reason it is so big is that I will use it as a haven from the public. I have a big recreation room with arcade games and a pool table and music—anything I find fun and relaxing.

My sudden fame has affected others too. My parents, my grandparents, my friends, all are experiencing something different in their lives because of their association with me. It may just be that they meet other famous people. My friends, in a sense, got drafted with me into the pros.

Luckily, most of my longtime friends have good jobs, so they're not living through me. If anything, I think I live through them. They're not scrutinized by the *Detroit News* or the *Detroit Free Press,* or the *Washington Post*. I genuinely enjoy hearing about their jobs. It's my connection to that thing that's called "the real world."

THE ROAD TO NOWHERE

Drugs and alcohol were certainly temptations when I grew up. There was peer pressure, and pressure from the outside. But I think kids today have it worse than I did.

I've got some good friends teaching high school now, and they back this up. Kids are drinking in junior high now. They're doing drugs sometimes even sooner than that. And sex? Everyone knows how peer pressure can influence that.

If I had a kid brother, sister, or cousin, I would tell them to wait. I would tell them not to rush

Standing in line during player introductions at the 1995 NBA All-Star Game with (from left to right) Scottie Pippen, Patrick Ewing, and Alonzo Mourning.

into something just because someone else is doing it. I would tell them to use their heads, and to call me when they need help.

I would tell them all this, and it would probably go through one ear and out the other.

That's because the younger you are, the more invincible you feel. So when I speak to kids in school, I don't preach. I show them.

I show them people like Brian Anthony (not his real name). When I was fourteen, he and I were the top two players in Reston. I did all the things to advance myself in the sport. I played AAU basketball in the summer, went to camps, got a national reputation going. Meanwhile Brian went to the playground every day and built a local reputation as a player. He and I were going to lead South Lakes High School to a state championship or two.

He never played at South Lakes. He never even made it to high school. He got involved in drugs, first using them, then selling them. He did time.

Here's the thing. He's not a bad guy, or mean. He victimized himself as much as others. I saw him after we won a championship at Duke, and he told me how proud of me he was. He told me he saw his dream come true through me. He wanted to make sure I kept going, saw through to my potential.

He told me not to mess up.

It was a sad moment. It was very emotional for him, and for me. And the irony was that it took place on a playground. Another irony is that when he tells kids he was once as good as Grant Hill, they probably don't believe him. But it's true. Everything that has happened for me could have happened for him.

He thought he was invincible. He was young. He had skill and talent and maybe dreams, but he lacked discipline and a work ethic. I kept away from things that would sidetrack my dreams and goals. And you should do that too, no matter what your goal is. You want to be a doctor, a lawyer, a politician? You have to have a plan, and then stick with it. You have to stay on track. You have to be focused.

You fall off the track, it's so hard to get back on it.

Brian is on the right track now, and he'll probably make something of his life. He's a good guy with a lot to offer. He figured that out the hard way. Don't ask *me* if drugs are a dead end. Ask *him*.

And when I talk about drugs, I'm talking

about alcohol too. It's a drug. It ruins lives and families and careers, even when taken by those of legal drinking age.

> Dreams only have a chance to live if fed the right things.

I don't drink. But my parents are social drinkers. They will go to parties or events, and have a drink or two. Obviously they haven't ruined their lives.

Obviously, they are not alcoholics.

Obviously, they are adults.

For the same reason a teenager should not carry a gun, a case of beer or bottle of whiskey is a bad idea too. How many kids are killed by cars driven by drunks every year? For that matter, how many adults are too?

How many teenage drinking sprees lead to drug experimentation or crime?

You don't need me to lecture you on this. Just look at the numbers.

But you're going to do what you want. So the next piece of advice is: "Be smart about it." If you're going to drink in high school, or even college, don't get behind the wheel. Don't take that next step into drugs. Don't take that next spiral downward.

Dreams only have a chance to live if fed the right things. Why do something that you already know could lead to the ruination of your dreams, your life?

That must be the greatest fear of every parent: the mistake that's impossible, or next-to-impossible, to fix. We've all had friends who have hurt themselves or others by drinking and drugs. We've all seen people who weren't as lucky as Grant Hill.

We've all seen people who weren't as lucky as Brian.

SEX: ARE YOU READY FOR YOUR LIFE TO CHANGE?

Some may object to following a chapter on drugs and drinking with one on sex. Sex is fun they'll say. Sex is natural. Sex is pure.

They must have just emerged from a couple decades of sleep.

Sex, especially without protection, can ruin lives or at least alter their paths. No one needs me to tell them that. No one needs Magic Johnson to tell them that, although his message carries a lot more weight than mine does.

I could give you a lot of reasons why sex in your teens is a big mistake. I could tell you that

I've seen lives detoured by unwanted parenthood, and we have all heard the horrible stories of AIDS.

Unfortunately, that won't stop anyone who wants to from trying. Despite all the evidence, it's clear that kids are still not scared. That invincibility factor again I guess.

It's not just kids. There are a lot of guys in the NBA, most college-educated, that are like that too. That just amazes me. Like teenagers, there are a lot of professional athletes who think they're invincible.

I'm really open with my parents, but I have always felt uncomfortable discussing my sex life with them. For one thing, if I tell my mother, she'll go and tell everybody.

I waited a long time before getting too deep into sex, and if you're smart, you'll wait too. Really, sex is something for adults. You have the rest of your life to be an adult. You have the rest of your life if you want to try alcohol.

Be a kid. Try to enjoy it. There are a lot of times I wish I could just be that kid again kicking a soccer ball around on that cul-de-sac.

THE ROOKIE

The day I was drafted, I looked at the Pistons roster and thought, "Playoffs." After the first day of training camp I thought the same thing, and I thought the same when we made some acquisitions over the season.

That was the first of many rookie mistakes. I aged a whole lot that year.

We got off to a good start, but I still don't know if that was because teams overlooked us, or because we were good. Hopefully, we'll find out this year that it was because we're good.

No doubt injuries stalled us, especially during the winter.

Holding my Rookie-of-the-Year trophy. I shared the award with Jason Kidd of the Dallas Mavericks.

For me it started in early December 1994 when I caught a bad case of the flu and Joe Dumars got it even worse. Until then we were playing about .500 and showing signs of coming together as a team.

There was a game against the Bulls in early December that became known as Black Friday. I was so sick they sent me home before the game. Joe was sick. Lindsey Hunter played and broke his ankle. From that point on, we started dropping like flies.

I got well, then I hurt my foot. Mark Macon was already out. Oliver Miller broke his hand. At times in January so many of us were hurt that we began to compete over the street clothes we wore on the bench. I think I looked nicest, but Mark West was an eleven-year veteran. He might have won by a thread.

We finally got our original team back together after the All-Star break, but whatever momentum we had gained early on was lost. We continued to lose, and we eventually cost Don Chaney his job.

I felt bad for him. He's a nice guy, and he was in a situation where he had to produce to save his job. And then he loses half the team he started with.

Dunking for two points against the
Indiana Pacers.

But just like players are judged a lot on their stats, coaches are judged on wins and losses, not how they did with an injured team. Coach K, for example, always had control. Whether it was that game against Kentucky when we were down with two seconds to go, or in the third quarter of a blowout, he had control of everything.

Coach Chaney was in a different situation. I don't know if that's just the difference between college and the NBA.

I thought a lot about that this past summer, and I was pretty upset with myself. I should have taken more of a leadership role, even if I was a rookie.

Last year, I worried too much about being liked. To be a leader you don't have to be liked. Christian wasn't always liked at Duke, and he didn't really care. If that's what happens this year, I won't mind that. I've been through a year when I've been liked and the team was terrible, and I'll take the reverse every year until my career is over.

I don't want to look back this summer and say, "If I had done this, or stepped up, or spoken out . . ."

THE FUTURE

I don't think discipline is going to be much of a problem this season. From what I know about our new coach Doug Collins, and from what I've heard from guys who have played for him, he's very tough, and very demanding.

Because of my friendship with his son Chris at Duke, I've known Doug for several years. Last summer, after he got the job, I was even included in discussions about team makeup and direction. I guess Doug values my opinion.

I know I value his. At Duke, Doug often took Chris and me out to dinner. The summer I spent rehabbing, he was around a lot, and we spent many hours talking basketball.

Doug has great understanding of the game and he communicates it well. When he explains something to you, or analyzes some problem you had with your game, he makes a lot of sense.

He's going to make us tougher. And he's hungry. Doug developed a young team at Chicago, and just when he was on the brink of a championship, he was let go.

I expect we will be a reflection of our new coach. I think we'll be tough. I have high expectations for the Pistons, but this year they are more realistic. I just want to improve, to be part of a plan that puts us on the path to a championship.

Doug has a plan. And I'm excited about being an integral part of that plan. Hopefully Allan Houston and I can do for Detroit what Joe Dumars and Isiah Thomas did in the last decade.

Maybe that's why Detroit has been so good to me already. I think prior to me coming, they were really looking for something. The Pistons had lost so many premier players in the last few years: Vinnie Johnson, Isiah Thomas, Bill Laimbeer, Dennis Rodman. The team had won those championships and then had fallen on hard times.

*My parents talk with Detroit Pistons coach Doug Collins,
whose son Chris was a teammate of mine at Duke.*

So here I come. Getting off to a quick start didn't hurt either. Once again, my timing was perfect.

Anyway, the fans here made me feel right at home. They're very loyal. Even when we didn't win a lot of games, they were very supportive. I can't imagine their reaction to the "Bad Boys" when they won consecutive championships. Hopefully, I'll find out firsthand.

It's not just Detroit either. Going around the country last summer, I received a positive response from people in many places. I don't know if it's the commercials, or my time at Duke, but I'm more recognized than I would have imagined.

It's on another level in Detroit, though. I think I came along to that city at a perfect time and I got off to a good start with the fans. I don't know why. Perhaps it's because I started a program with FILA that emphasizes academics as well as athletics. In order to participate in the program, you had to attend summer classes in math and English.

Once more for effect: Two parachutes are better than one.

FORTUNE

I am sometimes asked if money has changed me. I tell them, "Yes." Now instead of spending my parents' money, I'm spending my own.

That's pretty much the difference and I'll tell you why. My parents saw to it that I got everything I really needed, and that I was not wowed by wealth. We had fancy cars in the driveway, a nice house, famous and important friends. When I signed my first professional contract, I bought a GMC Truck and some casual clothes. I didn't really change.

But, boy, the world sure did.

Signing an autograph.

Earn a lot of money like that and you quickly begin to feel like a fish amidst a sea of hooks. Every guy you meet has a foolproof business deal. Women who don't even know you try to become your fiancée in five minutes. Try to go to a restaurant, or to a movie, or to anything, and you immediately become a huge, six-foot-eight disruption.

In that sense, I envy athletes from other pro sports. You wear a helmet in football and hockey, a cap in baseball. I'm six-eight. Even if I wasn't a basketball player, it's kind of hard to blend in.

But that's what I've tried to do. It's funny, but since I've been in the NBA, my lifestyle really hasn't changed. I don't live lavishly. For the most part I'm pretty simple. Anytime I meet someone new, they're usually shocked by my simplicity.

Because I've been fortunate to have everything I've always needed, money doesn't command my attention the way it does for some. Last year I moved into a rented condo, rented furniture, and lived out of boxes. For the whole season!

At the end of the season, I did buy a house, in a way as my commitment to being in Detroit and also as a concession to the changes around me. I can't go to an arcade and play video games without creating a scene. I can't shoot pool without creating a scene. I can't go to a club and listen to music without creating a scene.

Sometimes—a lot of the time—I don't want to create a scene. So now I have a house with an arcade and a pool table and my music. I can invite you over. Or I can just hang out by myself. I can just be Grant.

Don't get me wrong. Most of the time, I like the attention. I like what's happened to me. To see the commercials, a basketball with your name on it, a clothing line, your own shoe—it's hard to believe. I feel so lucky. It's been wonderful, more than I can imagine. So many things have happened to me already in one year that I couldn't even dream would happen over a career.

But I'm not greedy about that type of stuff. I want a championship. Just hearing my name announced at last year's All-Star Game gave me a taste of what could be. Being around all those great players, feeling as if I'm on the same level— I want that feeling every game.

I remember when I played against Jordan last season, I was in awe. I was so caught up being on the same court with Michael Jordan. I had only played against him when he was with the Dream

Matched against Michael Jordan in a late season game against the Chicago Bulls.

Team and I was part of a select group of college kids who scrimmaged against them. We were all in awe.

But then when I played against him last summer in a pickup game in California, it was different. I looked at him like he was anybody else, and I played better against him than I did back in the summer of 1992. Although he still dominated, I think he would say I was a different player.

I'm not a rookie anymore. The difference between now and last year is that I am a year wiser. I won't play in awe. I don't expect to make rookie mistakes. If you're smart, you learn from your failure. I like to think I'm smart. I like to think I learned a lot last season.

Michael will still score his points. But he'll work harder for them, and hopefully I'll get mine too. I know that I won't be in awe. I won't be like, "Oh my God, I'm on the same court as Michael Jordan."

Likewise with the All-Star Game. If I make it again, I won't think, "Oh my God, look at all these great players. What am I doing here?" I'll know why I was chosen.

THE DREAM TEAM

It had to be a prank. "Muhammad Ali wants to meet you," my mother said to me the day after the champ had wowed the world at Opening Ceremonies of the Centennial Olympics.

"Right, Mom," I said. "And I want to meet him too. And the Pope after that."

I never met the Pope, of course. But I will never forget meeting Ali and his 5-year-old son, Asaad. And judging from the reaction of my Dream Team teammates, I won't be alone.

Ali didn't want to meet me as much as his son did. His kindergarten teacher was a big fan of mine, and Asaad became a Grant Hill fan through him. It's funny how the world works.

Here's "The Greatest," a man beloved and recognized throughout the world, but he's just Dad to his son. Almost everyone in the world would want to meet Ali. His son? He wants to meet me.

It was almost scary. When I left, Asaad started crying.

I don't mind telling you that I felt like big man on campus that day. We met in the family center of the hotel, a ballroom converted to become a meeting place during the Olympics. I was late, as usual, and by the time I got down there, many of my teammates were sitting there, as was Ali and his son.

I thought everyone had met each other already, so I walked right over to Ali, shook his hand, and started talking to him. We were taking pictures, and all that time, the other guys on the team were just watching. No one had introduced them! They were sitting there, dying to meet him, and there I was just talking away!

Once that became clear, I introduced Ali to everybody who was there, as if he and I had known each other for a long time.

I was the man that day. You should have seen us, NBA All-Stars, acting like little kids as we shook his hand.

This was the day after what was perhaps the most moving Opening Ceremonies in Olympic history. I was as surprised as anyone when I saw Ali light the cauldron that night. I thought it was going to be another boxing champion, Evander Holyfield, who was born in Atlanta. When I saw Holyfield running out with the flame, I realized someone else would have to do it.

Holyfield had already run in and run around the track. He was getting tired.

Down on the Olympic Stadium field, we all started trying to figure out who it would be. When I saw Janet Evans hand the flame to Ali, I was stunned—just like everyone else watching.

A second or two later, I found myself and the whole U.S. basketball team going crazy. Everybody was screaming "Champ, Champ." Reggie Miller was recording everything with his video camera at ground level, and later we all practically attacked him with requests for copies. We told him, "Don't even speak to us again if you don't get us all copies of that tape."

The sight of Ali bonded everyone down on that field. Before that, we had been in our separate groups. All of the athletes had assembled across the street from Olympic Stadium, on the field at Fulton County Stadium. But for security reasons I guess, some of America's better-known athletes—Michael Johnson, Mike Powell, and the men's and women's Dream Teams—were gathered in a sky box.

That was my first inkling that the Olympics were not going to be the way I imagined they would be. I wanted to live in the Olympic Village, be part of the whole experience, but we were separated from the other Olympic athletes right from the beginning. We were the last athletes to come into the stadium, and because someone forgot to come and tell us when to leave the box, there was a gap between us and the rest of the athletes.

It probably looked as though we were prima donnas. It was just someone's mistake. You should have seen these prima donnas running down the ramp from the skybox and across the street, trying to catch the pack. I mean, we were sprinting.

Once we got into the stadium, heard all that noise, and saw the pageantry and 85,000 people in the stands, I wanted to keep running right around that track. I told Michael Johnson, "Man, it must be a great feeling to run in a place like this." He looked up and around, smiled, and said, "Yeah, it sure is."

Finally, after we walked around the track, we went over to where our other teammates were. If they were mad at us for that gap, they didn't show it. We took so many pictures, I feel like we met everybody on the U.S. team, and every coach. Then other countries came over, and pretty soon it got crowded, and very hot. As soon as Ali lit the torch and the swans flew overhead, we were rushed off, even as someone was singing. More security concerns I guess.

I think at that point I realized that I could not have lived in the Olympic Village. Isolating us in a hotel took away some of the Olympic experience for me, but I guess there was no other way. As the bombing a week later proved, terrorism was a real threat.

That bomb sucked some of the fun away for me. In some ways the Olympics were more than I expected, but in some ways they were much less. There were times I was so proud that I had to fight back tears. Other times I was scared enough to leave town or hole up in my hotel room.

There is no way to describe what it was like to win a gold medal and look at that crowd from the

victory stand. Hearing the national anthem, seeing the fans and the flags, pride just shot through
my body. I always felt that if I won a gold medal
I wouldn't go up there and do anything corny.
But that's exactly what I did.

I smiled. I waved. I gushed.

We played Argentina first, Yugoslavia last,
and were never in danger of losing. Yet I'll never
forget the feeling of nervousness, especially before
the first game. We knew we were better than the
team we were playing, but there was pressure on
us from fan and media expectations, and pressure
from ourselves. We were tight those first few
games, much different than the way we played in
practice, or during the exhibition games leading
up to the Olympics.

I can't speak for everybody, but for me, it was
the finality of it. This was something that started
a summer before, and all the talk, all the antici-
pation was finally over. Maybe this is how someone would be in the first game of a championship
series. You want to do well. So you're nervous,
excited, anxious—all the emotions you could pos-
sibly imagine.

It was a feel-out process. As it went on and we
started getting criticism from fans and the media,

we finally got some resolve. We finally said, "OK, we're tired of all this, let's go out and play our game." And we did. We started playing better and better, taking the ball to the hole, going after rebounds, playing more selfishly than before. I think we were all trying so hard to be good teammates at the beginning that we passed the ball too much, gave each other too much room.

Practices reflected that. I even twisted my knee the day before the gold-medal game when Charles Barkley landed on me. Although I could have played that final game, doctors advised against it, and I was reluctantly convinced of their wisdom by the Pistons and USA coach Lenny Wilkens. I suited up just in case though, and I celebrated with everyone afterwards. You don't always get everything you want out of life.

I got a gold medal though, and I contributed in every other game but the last two. I always thought people who won gold medals got too emotional up there on the stands. Having been up there, I now understand exactly why people react that way, especially if you have just won in an individual sport. The sacrifice involved to get there is just tremendous. Even Michael Johnson, who won gold medals in the 200-meter run and

400-meter run, couldn't hold it in. And he's about as cool as they come.

No one on our team cried, because you would have heard about it forever from Charles Barkley. But there was a part of each of us that wanted to. Even Charles did, I bet.

Charles may be cooler than Michael. Certainly he didn't let crowds, or bomb threats or anything else get in his way of enjoying the Olympics. I'd get in a van or a limo to go somewhere and there would be Charles, hat on head, walking through the middle of town.

If you said hi to Charles he'd say hi back. If you bothered Charles, he'd bother you back.

I wasn't nearly as bold, especially after that bomb went off in Centennial Park. After that, I didn't want to go anywhere.

My family and I were at Planet Hollywood with some friends when the bomb exploded that night. Planet Hollywood is on Peachtree Street, about five blocks away from the explosion, but we had no idea until somebody came and told us.

My parents, as always in a time of crisis, over-reacted.

They wanted to get back to the hotel as soon as possible. I wanted to go to a friend's house in

Alpharetta, an Atlanta suburb. My parents felt it was safer at the hotel, which had been secured that night by the military and U.S. intelligence, and which was patrolled by countless police and security. We came to call it "The Rock," the title of a prison movie with Sean Connery that was playing at the time.

Anyway, at first I let my parents talk me into going back to the hotel. We got in a limo and tried to return to the hotel, but we could only get within four blocks. The police had closed off the area surrounding the park while they treated victims and waited for federal investigators and bomb experts to arrive.

That was all I needed to see. I let my folks off and headed to Alpharetta, despite their objections.

We had one other bomb threat or scare at the hotel. The hotel was evacuated every time there was even a hint of a threat. Someone left a mysterious bag unattended somewhere, and the next thing you know, we were standing outside of the building.

My parents didn't let it take away from their fun. They went to Centennial Park after that, continued to attend games, and had a lot of fun with the families of other athletes staying at the hotel. My mom and Gary Payton's mom hit it off. My dad became a big fan of the women's team, and even stayed in Atlanta through closing ceremonies so he could watch their gold-medal game. They were the daughters he never had.

Me? I had a delayed reaction to the bombing. I wasn't scared the night it went off, but about two days later, it hit me. I realized what a target we were. After that, the only time I left was for practice or to get my hair cut.

Not Charles though. One of the best things about the Olympics was getting to know the guys on the team better. My mom found a friend for life in Payton's mom, and Gary and I got to know and like each other too. I grew up near David Robinson and knew his brother, Chuck, so there was already history there. But it will now be like a reunion when I see guys like Shaq, Penny, Reggie, and Scotty during the season.

Hakeem was right across the hall. There's class, and then there is this level above class. Hakeem is a notch above everybody else.

Charles? I don't agree with everything he says or does, but one thing I really respect about Charles is that he doesn't let anything change what he wants to do, or when he does it. That one day I saw him walking the street was a game day. That's part of his preparation, walking the street on game day, and nothing was going to stop him.

I'm more apprehensive I guess, which is why Charles saw a lot more of the Olympics than I did. I thought I would be able to get out more and I could have too, but it seemed like such a risk, and such a hassle. You had to round up security guards. You were advised to take a van or limo. Just getting a haircut a couple of blocks away was a hassle. The only reason I did that was because I had to. I didn't want to look bad on TV.

I've been going to that barbershop for years too, so the people there know me. I've been to Atlanta a lot because of basketball. In high school I played tournaments there. Playing for Duke, I went there for games against Georgia Tech, for ACC tournaments, and for NCAA tournament games. Now we play the Hawks there a few times each season.

I think that may have sapped some of the Olympic experience from me, even before I got the Centennial Park bomb jitters. Don't get me wrong—I think it was great to have the

Centennial Olympics in Atlanta. But I know Atlanta. I've seen everything there is to see in Atlanta.

I've never been to Sydney, Australia, site of the 2000 Olympics. I think if these Olympics had been in Sydney, I might have tried to get out more.

I plan to do that too. That's right—despite the fears, and the lack of mobility, and the pressure of expectations, I had a good time in Atlanta. There's no substitute for playing for your country and winning a gold medal. There's no other way to hang out and travel with other NBA All-Stars. The All-Star game is just a weekend, and a busy one at that. There's no time to work out with Karl Malone—what a weight-training machine—or to play video games with and against guys like Shaq and Penny. There's no time to play cards with Charles, and not enough time to share the laughs that he constantly provides.

For all those reasons, I would encourage any touted rookie to try out for the next team.

I will also tell him that he will have to get by me first.

Of the guys who were on the 1996 Dream

Team, maybe three guys might be around for 2000—Penny, Shaq, and me. Instead of the team puppies, like we were this time, we'll be the team leaders.

It's a scary thought. I'll be twenty-seven by then—a different player and, probably, a little different as a person too.

All of Grant Hill's proceeds and royalties from the sale of this book are being donated to children's and education-based charities.

I'LL GO TO BASKETBALL CAMPS NOW AND I'LL SAY, "HOW MANY OF YOU GUYS WANT TO PLAY IN THE NBA?"

Every single one of them will raise their hands. "How many guys want to play in college? How many guys want to start on your varsity team in high school?" The hands stay up.

Then I'll say, "Ten of you guys, out of two hundred, will play varsity basketball in high school. If you're lucky, one of you guys might play Division I college basketball. Those are the odds—maybe even less than that. That one person may have a chance at one of three hundred NBA jobs, although the odds again say probably not."

Every time I do this, kids stare at me dumbfounded. They don't realize that. I tell them, "The danger is not wanting to be like your heroes. The danger is in forgetting everything else to chase that. A dream is just that: something to shoot for. Arms in the sky, feet planted in reality."

Have another parachute. Have as many parachutes as you can. Then chase your dream with all your heart.

ADDED AT PRESS TIME, SPECIAL FOR THIS EDITION!

Grant Hill's Diary of the 1996 Olympic Dream Team—meeting Muhammad Ali; feeling the Olympic pressure; hanging with Barkley, Shaq, Penny, and other NBA stars; dealing with the aftermath of the bomb in Centennial Park; winning the gold; and more.